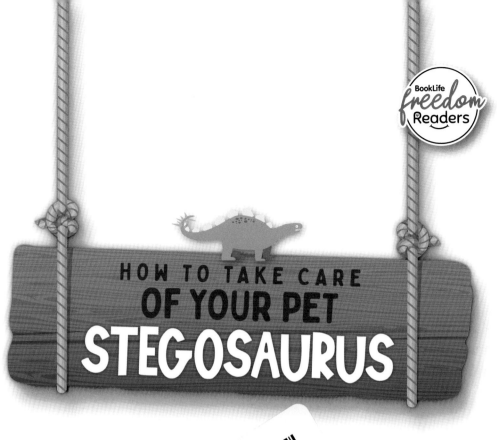

HOW TO TAKE CARE
OF YOUR PET
STEGOSAURUS

THE
OFFICIAL
F.O.S.S.I.L
GUIDE

BY KIRSTY HOLMES

BookLife
PUBLISHING

©2022
BookLife Publishing Ltd.
King's Lynn
Norfolk PE30 4LS

A catalogue record for this
book is available from the
British Library.

ISBN: 978-1-80155-131-1

Written by:
Kirsty Holmes

Edited by:
Madeline Tyler

Designed by:
Danielle Webster-Jones

All facts, statistics, web
addresses and URLs in this
book were verified as valid and
accurate at time of writing. No
responsibility for any changes to
external websites or references
can be accepted by either the
author or publisher.

BookLife
freedom
Readers

IMAGE CREDITS

CONTENTS

PAGE 4   F.O.S.S.I.L.

PAGE 6   Eggs

PAGE 8   Babies

PAGE 10   Growth

PAGE 12   Food

PAGE 14   Exercise

PAGE 16   Naming

PAGE 18   Washing

PAGE 20   Problems

PAGE 22   Tricks

PAGE 24   Questions

THE OFFICIAL FOSSIL GUIDE

F.O.S.S.I.L.

So, you're the proud owner of a dinosaur egg. Congratulations! Owning a pet dinosaur is a lot of hard work, but it is worth the trouble. Dinosaurs make excellent pets.

Per 1
Gn +1
C6/M7
P5/E2
M1 1.3

CONGRATULATIONS! IT'S A...
STEGOSAURUS!

If you are a first-time dinosaur owner, you probably have lots of questions. Never fear! This handy F.O.S.S.I.L. guide will tell you all you need to know. F.O.S.S.I.L. stands for the Federal Office of Super-Sized Interesting Lizards.

EGGS

Stegosaurus eggs are spherical. This means that they are round and the shape of a ball. They are about 11 centimetres wide.

11 CENTIMETRES

Stegosaurus eggs should be kept in a shallow nest, dug into some sand. Your egg will do well if it is kept warm, so build your nest in a sunny place.

BABIES

When it hatches out of its egg, Stegosaurus will be around the size of a kitten. Keep your pet in a closed, quiet room at first. They will be quite shy.

Feed your Stegosaurus mosses and ferns. Stegosaurus does not have a strong bite, so go ahead and feed your pet from your hands.

GROWTH

Your Stegosaurus will grow slowly and steadily. Babies are around the size of cats. Teenagers are around 5.6 metres long and 2.5 metres tall.

Adults can grow as long as 9 metres and weigh up to 7 tonnes. This is very heavy, so it might not be a good idea to let your Stegosaurus live upstairs.

FOOD

Stegosaurs are herbivores, which means they only eat plants. They have small teeth and a weak bite. Some of their favourite foods are grasses, mosses, berries, ferns and fruit.

Because its teeth are so small, your Stegosaurus might eat small stones. These are called gastroliths and roll around in the stomach to help the Stegosaurus digest its food.

EXERCISE

Your Stegosaurus will not need much exercise. They walk very slowly and spend most of the day eating. Try a gentle walk around the park if your pet is in the mood. Make sure your Stegosaurus does not step on your toes, though!

Stegosaurus has long spikes on the end of its tail. It is safest to stay at the front of your pet when going for walks to avoid being hit.

NAMING

Naming your Stegosaurus is very important when bonding with your pet. You could choose to use the first letter, S, when choosing a name. Can you think of any names that begin with S?

SOPHIE

You could use words that describe your Stegosaurus to name it instead. Stegosaurus has huge armoured plates and a spiky tail. Maybe you could call your Stegosaurus 'Spike'!

SPIKE!

WASHING

It is important that you keep your pet clean, especially between its plates. You will need lots of cleaning equipment such as goggles, a scrubbing brush, a cloth and a bucket. A ladder could also be useful to reach the top of your Stegosaurus!

After your Stegosaurus is clean, make sure to carefully polish the plates to a nice shine with some polish and a cloth. This will bring out the colours.

PROBLEMS

Stegosaurus has a small brain — only about as big as a walnut. This means that they are not very bright and can easily get into trouble. We recommend keeping a close eye on your pet.

One problem with herbivores is that they make a lot of gas. That is another good reason to stay at the head end of your pet at all times.

GROSS!

TRICKS

As your Stegosaurus will not be very bright, it will not learn tricks easily. However, you can try climbing onto its back using its armoured plates.

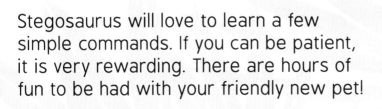

Stegosaurus will love to learn a few simple commands. If you can be patient, it is very rewarding. There are hours of fun to be had with your friendly new pet!

QUESTIONS

1: Does your Stegosaurus egg need to be kept warm or cold?

2: How wide are Stegosaurus eggs?
- **a)** 2 centimetres
- **b)** 11 centimetres
- **c)** 300 centimetres

3: What does Stegosaurus eat?

4: What is a gastrolith?

5: What would you like to do with your Stegosaurus? Make a to-do list.